Anthology No.2

Brampton Poets 2020

Copyright © 2020 Brampton Poetry Group

*The right of the Brampton Poetry Group to be identified as the Author of the Work has been asserted by them in accordance Copyrights, Designs and Patents Act 1988.
The Copyright for each poem resides with its author.*

First Published in 2020 by Brampton Poets 2020

Apart from any use permitted under UK copyright law, this publication may only be reproduced, stored in a retrieval system, or transmitted, in any form, or by any means, with prior permission in writing of the publisher or, in the case of reprographic production, in accordance with the terms of licenses issued by the Copyright Licensing Agency.

All characters and events in this publication, other than those clearly in the public domain, are fictitious and any resemblance to real persons, living or dead, is purely coincidental.

Print ISBN: 978-1-8380177-0-5

Note:

This collection of poetry was compiled during the COVID-19 lockdown period. Our thoughts, of course, are with all those near and far that have been affected by this awful pandemic. Any profits, beyond publication costs and the associated overheads of the Brampton Poetry Group will be gifted to an NHS related Charity within our area – with our thanks and in awe of their contribution!

Brampton Poets 2020

CONTENTS

Preface 7

The Poets 9

The Poems

David Bamford 19
  September 19
  Winter landscape 20
  Snowdrops 22
  Spring. An apostrophe 24
  June 26
  Landscape 28
  The land 30
  October 32
  Autumn 34
  Howgills 35
  The garden in early February 36
  Metamorphosis 38
  Mud-caked Me 39
  Sign Language 42
  Solitude 44
  Life in the Coronaverse 46
  Swallows 48

David Hurd 49
  Harrop Tears 49
  Snow 50
  Events 51

   Water ways..52
   Resolve..56
   H$_2$O..57
   Widow's words...60
   Childs play...61
   Mind's eye..62
   A Powerful Dilemma..................................64
   On the Bridge..67
   Joint Effort...68

Ena Hutchinson 70
   Joy Complete...70

Gilbert Hutchinson 72
   "Will Not Come Back"................................72
   Main Street Keswick 1985.........................73
   Wedding Day 74

Ruth Kershaw 76
   Full Circle 76
   Rejoining...80
   Back to Square One 82
   Fatal Attraction. 83
   The Strangers 84
   Into The Van...86
   The Man In The Van. 86
   Oh Help....................... 88
   Knotty Stuff...89
   Swim No More, My Lady............................90

John S Langley 93
- Surprise Package 93
- The Wheels on the Bus 94
- Carlisle Fish and Chips 96
- Cat Sick 98
- The Rapper 100
- First Steps 101
- Mary Queen of Scots 102
- Bewcastle Cross 104
- Reivers 106
- Brampton Roman Camp 108
- A Bridge Too Far 110
- The Dipper 113
- A Virtual Trip to Martindale 114
- Family Pieces 117
- There Will Come Another Spring 120

Doreen Moscrop 123
- Dawn o'er Blencathra 123
- The Winter Lullaby 124
- The Wayfarer's Friend 126
- The Geltsdale Shepherd 128
- The Mardale Shepherd 130
- Striding Edge 132
- The Winter Robin 133
- My Secret Tarn 134
- The Miner's Day 136
- The Magic Tarn 137
- The Carpets of Spring 138

Jean Taylor 140
  My Favourite Book 140

Stuart Turner 142
  Beach Love 142
  Autumn Fields 146
  Early Winter Scene 147
  Moorland 150
  On Harrow Scar 154
  Death of a Friend 157
  Winter Owls 158
  Lines Written to the Wind 160
  Talkin Fell 162
  Upper Geltsdale 164
  Upper Geltsdale Winter 166

Space for poems of your own 167

Poetry Anthology No.2

Acknowledgements

Our heartfelt thanks are due to the *Cottage Coffee community* for the financial assistance that made the publication of the first anthology possible. We have now been inspired to attempt a second.

Brampton Poets 2020

Preface

Brampton Poets is a name assumed by a group of people who meet monthly in the Community Centre in Brampton. The group was born out of a Poetry Breakfast event in the Theatre by the Lake in Keswick in 2016, under the umbrella of Words by the Water, at which people were invited to gather for breakfast and to read poetry: their own or that of others.

Ena and Gilbert Hutchinson, Brampton residents, brought the concept back to Brampton, contacted a number of acquaintances whom they knew to be interested in poetry and suggested adopting the same format on a monthly basis.

The group meets at 10 a.m. on the first Thursday of every month, enjoys breakfast and chat for half an hour, then reads poetry for a period of 45 minutes to an hour.

The idea of this second anthology was prompted by the meetings of the group.

Brampton Poets 2020

Poetry Anthology No.2

The Poets

David Bamford

David Bamford came to live in Lanercost in 2010 after having worked in education in South America for 22 out of the previous 25 years. He returned to UK to retire, but soon found himself working part time at Austin Friars School in Carlisle, teaching Spanish, until they ran out of hours for him. Shortly after retiring for the second time, he was offered a few hours teaching French at Hayton C of E Primary School, which he loves.

David has had a love of poetry for as long as he can remember and numbers poets among his forebears. He is also a Reader in the Church of England, an active participant in theatrical activities and an inveterate writer of letters to the Cumberland News.

He sees poetry as a form of written expression that captures a moment of inspiration and fixes it as a kind of epiphany (and he hopes that doesn't sound too pompous!)

David Hurd

David Hurd was born in 1940 and lived for the first ten years of his life in Scarborough. He then lived for five years in Wetheral. At the age of fifteen he joined the army and trained as a cartographic draughtsman. He served twenty years in the army before being made redundant.

David worked at Bartholemew's in Edinburgh, then at Metal Box in Carlisle. He then worked for a small reproduction company, doing art and film work for various printers until he was made redundant again at 55.

He then spent four years at the Cumbria College of Art and now produces three-dimensional creations using clay, welded metal and fibreglass, carved wood and stone. He also spends more time writing poetry, to which he was first alerted before leaving Irthing Valley school.

Ena R. E. Hutchinson

Ena was born in Harrogate Golf Club in 1936 where her parents were living as Steward and Stewardess. During World War II Ena, a younger brother and two younger cousins were all brought up together as one family, with grandparents and aunt, while the fathers were serving abroad.

On leaving secondary school, Ena attended Harrogate Technical College for Catering. Leaving there at 16, she undertook a two-year managerial course in London with J Lyons & Co. before returning to Yorkshire to be with her grandmother after her grandfather's death. Ena married her first husband in 1958 and had two sons and, later, six grandchildren.

With a career as a self-employed caterer, Ena moved North to Preston in 1964 and then into the Borders. In the early 1980s, Ena ran the Cathedral Buttery - as it was in those days.

Ena met Gilbert in 1985. They were married in 1986 and moved to Brampton in 2002. They shared a love of walking, nature, books and music, and Ena came to appreciate poetry. Following trips to 'The Theatre by the Lake' in early 2016, the idea of a Brampton Poets Group was formed and, following encouragement, launched.

Robert Gilbertson Hutchinson

Gilbert was born in 1919 in Carlisle and had two older brothers. He had a love of cricket and as a boy wanted to be a groundsman at Edenside cricket club.

As a teenager he joined the Border Regiment Territorial Army and was on manoeuvres in France when World War II was declared. During the war he served as wireless operator in France, Tobruk, Middle East and India. He spent many a leave in Keswick with his uncle Bob Graham - the fell runner who, in 1932 ran 42 peaks in 24 hours at the age of 42 (known as the Bob Graham Round).

After leaving the Army Gilbert went to Teacher Training College. His subject was History. He was an avid reader and loved poetry, which he wrote. He also had a great love of the countryside. After a teaching post in Carlisle Gilbert moved first to London and then on to a Secondary School in Gloucestershire as Head Teacher, and later to Church School in Devon.

Due to health issues he took early retirement. After the death of his first wife he returned to his beloved Carlisle and the Cumbrian hills. In 1985 he met Ena, who shared similar interests, and they married in 1986. Gilbert died on the 14th December 2017.

Ruth Kershaw

Ruth has lived in Brampton for 50 years. She was born in Rochdale, but, due to her father's promotions on the railway, found herself in Halifax by the time she was 10. Here she stayed until she had gained School Certificate. Now at the northern end of the chain, Ruth thinks of herself as a Pennine woman and revels in their wildness. She has walked the Pennine Way.

A long period of bedrest (age 6 rheumatic fever) gave time to indulge in Arthur Mee's encyclopedia, the Poetry and Natural History sections laying foundation for lifelong interests.

She is indebted to her English teacher for encouraging her to write essays but did not venture into poetry until 2013 when she enjoyed a Poetry Course at Stones Barn, Roweltown, North Cumbria, led by Ian Duhig. Immediately "hooked" she has attended 2 more of the same.

A retired Methodist Minister, she finds poems easier than sermons.

John S Langley

John Langley was born and raised in the North East of England and has two brothers, three sons and only one wife.

After qualifying as a Chemical Engineer he was lucky enough to work around the world on various projects before moving into Consultancy and finally becoming his own Company.

He has enjoyed writing creatively all his life, a trait that was not always appreciated whilst at school, but the disciplines of Technical Report writing put something of a dampener on this for about 30 years.

Now settled back in the North he has time to write with freedom and experimentation and has even built up enough courage to admit to being an Author and a Poet.

Doreen Moscrop

Doreen was born and educated in Brampton and has now returned here to live. Having had a varied career in accountancy, shepherding, and office management, she has always maintained a great affection for the countryside and the Lake District. She began walking seriously in Lakeland in 1994, completing the Lake rounds and then the highest mountains, in preparation for her charity walks of Snowdon and Ben Nevis. Her final challenge was to visit all 214 named tarns in the National Park. These pursuits were her inspiration for returning to her painting and poetry composing pastimes.

Jean Taylor

Jean lived in Hethersgill Cumbria for 25 years and then in Brampton for the past 3 years. She was born in Liverpool in 1932 and joined Martins Bank (which later became Barclays Bank) in 1948 at the age of 16 – the youngest person to join. In 1954 Jean joined the Wrens and worked in The Admiralty Building in London. Having left the Wrens in 1956 to get married Jean had 4 children and worked alongside her husband running their own dairy business in Liverpool until they both retired aged 61 and moved to Cumbria.

The poem in this Anthology is her first ever poem - written at the age of 87!

Stuart Turner

Stuart Turner was born on 7th May 1942 in Newcastle and spent his childhood in Consett, a steel town in County Durham (the Steel Works closed in 1980). He belongs very much to the Christian family and the upholding of Christian traditions. He attended Annfield Plain Secondary Modern School and was introduced to Literature, in particular, by his Headmaster, who was a brilliant man with the iconic name of W.E.Gladstone.

He started writing poetry in 1962 after he joined the Royal Air Force and concentrated more specifically on this after the millennium in 2000 when he had more time after raising a family. He has engaged in both verse and prose, and his writing usually focuses on a mixture of nature and human interaction.

Poetry Anthology No.2

The Poems

David Bamford

September

Sometimes, a poem is suggested by a single word. So it was one September day when I went outside and felt the cut of an early frost.

Sharp
the hard metallic bite of early autumn
a steel-cold sky now shorn of birds
glass-brittle blades of grass erect unmoving
crisp-edged leaves that shiver
crumbling at a touch
stillness
lack of motion
washing hangs inert upon the line
refusing stubbornly to dry
dead-headed roses
no longer fragrant-scented
unornamental even
raised-armed skeletons wondering what. . ?
meanwhile the garden curls
to enter sleep
the year is on the turn

Winter landscape

Winter can be very forbidding in Cumbria; cold, dark and long. The lifeless landscape holds little comfort. Yet, occasionally, there can be a flash of brightness amidst the gloom.

Stark
Sterile
Stiff.
Skeletal trees standing rigid,
static sentries defying advancing armies
of a threatening storm.
Ragged remnants of recent snow
extruded from a constipated sky.
Dirty white on black,
monochrome contrast in a winter landscape,
lacking lustre
lacking colour
lacking . . . . anything.
Nothing stirs.
Frozen folds of fields,
of meadows.
Ice on cattle troughs,

puddles, surface hard as bone,
dead and ironed skulls
raise frozen eye sockets, sightless,
frigid to the world.
Frost holds in icy grip
what once was fresh and green,
ripe, fertile, quivering with life,
now a mingling of white and brown,
grey on black,
lifeless, cold,
lacking motion,
devoid of warmth,
a warmth that's gone.

In the garden a flash of fire,
a fleeting flame of robin's breast,
as a bird hops in to feed.
As if on cue and for an instant, before it sets,
The sun creeps down below
its leaden curtain
and bathes the ground in light.

Snowdrops

My wife and I returned to live in the UK in 2010 after a number of years in South America. At the end of our first winter, the sight of snowdrops made me think how my mother would have loved to know where we had come to live. The snowdrop was her favourite flower.

Patches, carpets of white, where was
but a short while since another white.
Under trees, in churchyards and at roadsides,
the year's novitiate, heads bowed
in bashful reverence, bridesmaids
clad in white, awaiting the triumphant
golden trumpet of the daffodil, the bride of spring.
Elfin caps, their pointed petal tips
bent towards the earth from which they've sprung,
bearing the frosty bite of winter's dying breath.
Unmoved, unmoving, huddled close together,
safe in their numbers, like penguins in a blizzard.

The daintiest of flowers announcing coyly
that we may now leave off our winter lethargy.

Poetry Anthology No.2

Spring. An apostrophe

Although we have a good deal of rain in Cumbria, fine spring days are always warmly appreciated. Nature has such personality here, by no means always benign. In fact, she is often known to be relentlessly hostile. It's good, therefore, to speak to her and let her know that her more attractive aspects are always noticed and welcome.

Hallo, spring.
Are you just passing through again,
or have you come to stay awhile
this time?
Winter's long and agonising farewell
that would not let it go,
would not release its iron clasp
that held us to its damp and shivering breast,
is now a fading echo on the breeze.

Today, this afternoon,
your warming beams of sun
caress the garden.
Shoots poke through the not so long since sodden soil.
A cacophony of rooks
caws raucously from lofty nests.
A pair of collared doves,
returned from they know where,
strut with stately beigeness on the lawn,
picking food from others' leavings.

Thank you, spring,
for showing us your face.
Thank you for the warmth,
the growth,
spikes of perennial plants
now showing, wondering
if, this time,
you're really going to stay a while.
Please be assured
you're always welcome.

June

June is a notoriously fickle month, unable to make its mind up whether it belongs in summer or in some depressingly wet other season. At its best, particularly as gardens come alive, it can produce magnificence.

Sunbeams burst midst shrubs and bushes.
Fluffy bumblebees buzz buzzily among the blooms,
caressing purple flowers of iris,
cobalt-coloured cornflowers, alliums, pink and purple aquileji.
Butterflies flutter in crazy flight from plant to plant,
white wings among the yellows, mauves and greens.

Poppies and peonies parade their reds and pinks,
vying with each others' proud displays.
Profusion and effusion, sound and joyful blossoming.
Blackbirds trill their English garden song;
bluetits speed from feeding station to grub-rich ground
to nesting box,
to feed impatient hungry young
that tweet, gape-beaked,
receiving eagerly what caring parents carry home.

Nature bursts with life,
the legacy laid down by long wet winter,
blessed with interest by warm spring multiplied,
now exploding in the heat of early June,
as flower heads reveal their beauty.
The drone of mowers complements
the harmony of nature's song.
Sheds are emptied, painted, cloches cleaned,
pots sorted, thrown away or kept.
And gardeners face the challenge,
don gloves to take the gauntlet
thrown down by nature.
"You'll never beat me, but we can work together
to create a thing of beauty."

Landscape

Seen from a train, the Cumbrian landscape has a character all its own. Unmistakeable. It's always a joy, at any time of year, to feel that one's returning home.

Drystone walls,
sweeps of pasture, holding sheep
that idly stand and slowly move
across the vastness.

Rolling folds of dark brown fields
yielded to the turning of the plough,
tumbling becks, ghylls, incisions in the land,
scars sabre-slashed,
trimmed with tufts of vegetation.

A striding shepherd with his dog
plods, prodding with his crook.
Gumboots, waxed jacket, flat cap
in muted country check,
the uniform of one wedded to the land,
at one with his vocation,
dependent on the elements,
the sheep he knows by name,
as they
know him by his voice and smell,
and trust his call.

Poetry Anthology No.2

The land

The reality of climate change is inescapable and can no longer be ignored. The land and its resources are only renewable up to a point, and those who tell us, constantly, that we have now reached the point of no return can no longer be accused of alarmism. The devastation caused by bush fires in Australia at the end of 2019 and the beginning of 2020 have drawn worldwide attention to the vulnerability of the environment which is lent to us for our responsible care and enjoyment.

The land, by turns benign and hostile,
smiling, beguiling,
snarling, baring teeth and biting back
against abuse.
Always in motion,
giving birth and growth,
providing, yielding sustenance.
Bounteous fountain of abundance,
to be cared for, tended and enjoyed
since Adam took on his stewardship.

Have we lost this legacy
with pesticides,
massive modification, mechanisation
and materialistic exploitation?

As a child that's nurtured will repay the care,
a land that's fed will reproduce.
If it's damaged, raped and devastated,
squeezed of all its goodness
and left barren,
it will have no more to give,
so it
and we
will die.

October

Although autumn marks the beginning of the end of the year, it seems to contain an onrush of energy as fruit flourishes and is dropped or picked. As a cycle comes to its end, another begins, and the splendour of October holds promise for the future.

Earth exudes a fragrance,
loam-laden, heavy
with mouldering vegetation,
as decay and decomposition
return to earth
what earth produced.
Earth to earth
to sprout and flower again.

Heaps of leaves heave,
rich with autumn colours,
copper, russet, golden brown.
Worms gorge and surfeit
deep in the warm-reeking mass.
Fertility lies dormant,
yet incubates, regenerates.
Silent nature nurtures,
lays foundations,
a cyclical progression;
birth, growth, maturity,
decay and death
and then . .
rebirth.

Tips poke from bulbs of hyacinth
and paperwhite
in time for Christmas.

And in the Church
a rich abundance
of what's been cut
and picked and dug,
cleaned off and offered here
to feed the needy
and then begin again,

while in the garden,
dead growth is trimmed, cut off and burnt.
What's left is left to rest, recover,
as energy goes back into the roots,
defying winter's coming chill
and, in the spring
to come back
stronger.

Autumn

Weather, of which we get a lot in Cumbria, often prompts musings in a reflective and poetic vein. The transit of the year encourages this, and this is one of the reasons for which I often find myself writing about the weather and nature. Obviously, I am but one in a long and valued line of wordsmiths who do this.

Bunching clouds,
the furrowed brows of winter's heralds,
build mountains against the pale grey sky
that shrinks away
and beats the limp retreat
of a summer that never really was.
An alarum of rooks
rises, wheels, caws in cacophonous panic
as distant thunder growls.

Nature assumes a cloak of menace
as, from billowing storm clouds,
begin to fall
fat drops of rain.
They smack on window panes,
explode in tiny diamonds
and among the trees keens a quickening breeze.

Time to put on an extra layer,
light the fire
and think of crumpets,
hot,
with melting butter.

Howgills

Frost casts an icing sugar dusting
on morning surfaces,
slanting sunlight highlights humps and furrows,
slashed wounds of darkness
scrape charcoal-coloured clefts
of ghyll and force.

Recumbent elephants,
humped flanks soak up light
beneath an ice-blue sky,
green and brown below,
salt-and-pepper-dashed with sheep,
through burnished copper-bracken,
to beige above,
where grass, scorched and burnt
by winter's blowtorch,
slumbers in late hibernant state,
waiting for a sigh of spring
to coax it back to life.

The garden in early February

A frosted surface cracks,
a shoot pokes coyly through,
a stalk of hellebore
yawns and stretches,
opens a shy bud to test the air.
Is it warm enough to wake,
to view the stone-hard earth
that still sleeps round about?

Last autumn's fallen leaves
have lain, a blanket unraked and undisturbed,
have formed an insulating cover
between the earth and upper cold.

Primroses, not sure what's happened to the seasons,
present wide-open eyes of startled yellow,
and sprouts of green appear
on bare hydrangea twigs,
while spears of allium
bristle in the shade
and even tulips now reach skyward.

Time to unlock the shed,
Take out the tools
And get to work once more.

Poetry Anthology No.2

Metamorphosis

A cocoon, a winding sheet, a shroud.
The dormancy of death enshrines a form
that lived to eat
and drink and desecrate,
devour, defoliate,
digest and defecate,
then, surfeited, slip into slumber
while nature does her work,
secretes the shroud
around the sated form
that sleeps that stage away.
Inert, immobile,
within the protecting pod,
confined, constrained, constricted.
A body in a coffin of its own creation.
Dead, until. . .
the day of Resurrection.
A body bursts
and struggles forth,
transformed.
To stretch, to squeeze, to stagger out
on fragile, pin-thin legs,
uncrease its wings
to expand and quiver,
feel the air,
the medium that has become its home,
allows for flight,
as a buttterfly takes wing.

Mud-caked Me

The Hadrian's Wall path to the west of Carlisle crosses stretches of farmland. Much of this is inhabited by cattle, so, when it rains, which, in Cumbria, occurs with frequency, the ground becomes very muddy. One day in March 2020, I was walking this stretch when, on losing my balance, I found myself sitting in what must have been the muddiest part of the field through which the path led me.

Walking across a muddy field –
a very muddy field –
I approached a little stone-built bridge
across a trickling watercourse.
At either end, a spring-hinged gate
of bright-fresh timber, recently installed,
stood guard.

I could see no way to circumvent
the patch of mud
upon whose edge I'd halted.
I took a step
and then another,
paused, took stock
and thought.
'Was this wise?'
I wondered.
And yet I saw no other course.
'Returning were as tedious as go o'er.'

I pulled a boot up through the squelching ooze
and lost my balance,
fell backside first
into a soft brown water-heavy porridge,
cold.

I sat there.
How do I get up?
No lever,
I sat and thought,
dampness seeping through
onto my lower half.
The only course,
turn over on my knees
and push
upwards on my walking pole.

The pole sank,
as did my arms,
up to the elbows,
but I stood up,
a mud-caked zombie,
feeling stupid.

Out I squelched
onto the flag before the bridge.
Firmer ground.

I swung the gate,
leaving mud upon the shining slats,
muddy boot-prints on the stones,
through the second gate and up the slope.
Only seven more miles to walk.
The mud will dry
and I, once more,
will seem to look
almost human.

Sign language

The sign says
'Baby changing in the disabled toilet.'
Is it the toilet that's disabled,
or those for whose use
it is designed
in some way
physically disadvantaged?
Is one invited to (ex)change one's baby
or merely make him
– or her –
sanitarily acceptable?
Posteriorly comfortable?
Fragrantly cuddlable?
Or merely dry and clean, unsoiled?

I also wonder, when I see a sign
that indicates 'Permissive Footpath',
whether 'tis a footpath
that is somehow loosely moralled,
turning Nelson's eye
to misuse, abuse or any other use
than that for which it was intended.

Can things inanimate grant concession?
Allow unhindered passage? (No,
I'm not referring here
to babies' bowels and bladders, so
please excuse the unintended
ambiguity).

The owner of the land
traversed by the mentioned footway
may be permissive
in his attitude
in granting latitude
to take that way
so long as we obey,
of course, the country code.

The bottom line,
I s'pose, is that we know
where we are going and why,
what we're doing
and by what right,
to keep our noses, feet
and parts unmentionable clean.

Solitude

Walking alone in the countryside during the time of social distancing awakens the senses to one's surroundings and also to the absurdity of enforced apartness.

On my own,
the sky and clouds for company
like flocks of sheep
moving fluffily across the sky.

Dips and humps of green and, over there,
the spire of a distant church upon a hill.
And trees,
beech and birch
and ancient oak,
that filter sunlight
to the ground.
Feet grind the beech mast
to crunch like day-old crisps beneath my boots
among the tarnished copper of past years'
leaves.

No one else about,
then suddenly, at once,
three people whom I know.
I'm hailed by one who's running past;
The others, with a dog, stop.
We talk
at and from a distance
and then
continue on our way.

The breeze stirs,
birds sing,
a wandering bumble bee
weaves its way across my path.
Does nature wonder
what has happened to humanity,
that people used to throng
now seek to keep their distance?
Humanity itself knows not
what has become of it.
What has become of it?
Where are we bound?
For bound we are, not free,
to stay within our space
and keep our distance
from each other.

Life in the Coronaverse

A time of lockdown, living life in slow motion. The car was put under a cover, mainly to protect it from bird droppings, hardly ever used. Existence was eked out; we ate less, and less frequently, did not go out, except for the statutory period of exercise, like prisoners, but with no walls. Many wondered whether life would be the same. This was a new 'normal,'

Horizons shrunk
to a limit walkable
within an hour,
there and back again.

When meeting others on the road
or path,
we do the Levite Shuffle,
the Priestly Sidestep,
move aside, pass by
upon the other side,
create a gap two metres wide.
Of course, we nod a greeting,
smile,
pass the time of day
and comment on the weather.

Today, I should have been
leaving on a pilgrimage,
but, like much else,
it's now postponed,
pending.
Pending what?
A moving on.

We won't go back.
We can't,
for the world has changed
and we are not the same.
When we get through,
we shall be sadder, yes,
but maybe wiser too.

Swallows

The swallows have returned,
piping, wheeling, diving, swooping,
scythe-bladed wings carving swathes across
the sky.

Spitfires, flown by pilots high on speed,
exulting in the exuberance of flight.
With unerring accuracy
they zoom through ruined buildings' blind-
eyed paneless windows,
through open doors of barns.
playing aerobatics with each other,
vying for insects that they catch upon the
wing.

Pure energy, sheer delight in flight
between the green of fields, the blue of
heaven,
bringing us the promise of a summer
that may be,
once more,
perhaps.

David Hurd

Harrop Tears

Murmuring winds and sighing breeze, that wisps the evening clouds,
Wraps peaks and tree-tops, vales and hills, gently in its shrouds.
Late afternoon, when winter sun, shines weak with orange glow,
Sets the hills aflame with light, and gilds the waters' flow,
Cascading over glistening rocks, to froth in deep dark pools,
Encrust the ponds, the stalks and grass, in icy winter's grip,
To stalactite, in crystal form, the melt of mid-day's drip,
As cool the evening blaze the sky, azure and crimson glow,
Then night befall to grey the scene, as home reluctant go.

Snow

Flurry down in silence see the crystal snowflakes fall,
Blanketing the city with its chilly winter call,
Painting grey the heavens, coating white the earth below,
The silent drift of seasons, fetches winter's wings of snow.
Its lazy downwards flutter, or frenzied spiral whirls,
Appliqués bricks and branches then slowly melts to pearls,
It cameos the roof tops, the hedges, ditches walls,
The eerie sound of silence, as noiselessly it falls.

Events

Not only do you wash the cups, the plates, the knives and forks,
But also you must pick it up, from where he's been for walks,
For is he not a year abouts, and doing very well,
For have you never heard the shouts if he cannot feed himself,
He sits up there all prim and proud, a spoon held in his hand,
Proceeds to spread it all around,"look Mummy ain't it grand"
Potatoes here, a carrot there, some kidney on the floor,
When finally you pick it up, he doesn't want no more.

Water ways

The gurgling of the stream at birth, from the
   saturated sod of conception,
To the trickling into adolescent growth, from flood
   to flow transition,
The childish babbling of the brook, which slowly
   starts meandering,
Via ditches, drains, and minnowed creeks, on its
   downwards trek now wandering.
The creek with raindrops to swell its girth, with
   ditches and drains to broaden,
No longer aimless, has set its sights through
   banks which guide and cordon,
Sister rivulets join in the flow to stream along
   together
From bogs of peat to pastures new, to leave behind
   the heather.

Wooded banks now hide its growth, o'er pebbles
   and stones it tumbles,
It broadens out and speeds its flow, cascades with
   a voice which now rumbles.
Wider now and river wise, it flows on its current
   soaring,
Over boulders now it splashes and plunges,
   surging onwards downwards seeking.
Under bridges which span, to test its flow, over
   chasms which tumble it headlong,
To waterfall into depths' dark glow, almost the
   salmon's swansong,
Through reed, weed and iris, it rushes past, each
   village and town is touching,
Via man's domain, where city waste, joins the flow
   in the form of a douching,

Poetry Anthology No.2

To see to seawards the salty tang, hear the waves
on the foreshore pounding.
To intermingle with the salt and join in their
thunderous sounding,
Waters fresh and salt united now, wave together in
undulation,
Cold at first, this saline yoke that wraps itself
round the nation
From the arctic wastes of ice and chill, through
the tropics of corn or cancer,
Where seas and oceans are never still and white
the wave topped prancer,
Where ebb and flood the waters flow, relate the
moonlight's motion,
Waves from the windward's oceans spread, always
moving this saline potion.

Pounding this sphere from east to west, bear
flotsam and froth with each wave,
Fish or insect, man bird or beast, serves to all as a
watery grave.
The tropical sun beats the golden sand from the
cloudless azure sky,
Evaporate from limpid pools, leaving starfish,
poached, parched and dry.
Ozone rising to drift on the breeze, 'neath the
sun's relentless beating,
Where palm trees rustle, as their leaves applaud
the wind in a formal greeting.
Stratus, nimbus and cirrus clouds, distilled in the
air as a vapour,
Winds like forties roaring south conveying their
airborne moisture,

Spreading the worldwide sea of sky, which clouds
    the land's formation,
Where baked beneath their canopy, awaits the
    earth in parched expectation.
Dark and sullen clouds that form, in bible black
    dark wonder,
Parched the landform, scorched below, press the
    clouds to thunder.
Drizzling rain comes pattering down; its cargo now
    is falling,
Sigh in grateful praises be, relief the drought lands
    calling.
Now dampened down the swirling dust, dry
    branches their leaves extending
To drink and quench the season's thirst, the
    drought at last is ending,

Once failing crops now full and flush form a
    harvest fit for reaping.
The plough-share slices through the clay, where
    the lifeblood now is seeping.
Sap now flows through strengthened limbs
    through roots and trunk a-surging,
Yet still the rain-clouds linger there, more of
    themselves disgorging
Down the hillside watershed, to sate the valley
    floor
Sufficient that no more will seep, earth's coffers
    full to store.
From here the surplus finds release, to trickle and
    meander,

To flood again the dry bed stream, enact again the wonder,
From sated sod, down to the sea, via streams and rivers boulder
Where fresh with salt, is tied the knot re-quench the tropic smoulder.
Fleece together and dust their way, repaint the heavenly splendour,
Till breezes push the laden clouds, to again, shed their cargo of wonder.

Resolve

Forgive me if I'm morbid; ignore me when I'm grim,
Permit me my self-pity for I'm just as sick as him,
But he seems not to notice, his pains don't seem to last,
We both have violent spasms, but his seem quickly past.
Next time I'm pushed beside him, I'll ask why should that be?
We both are fellow sufferers, and he's as sick as me,
Yet he seems always cheerful he never moans nor greets,
His cheerful friendly outlook he shares with all he meets.
"Excuse me, Sir, I've noticed, forgive me if I'm rude,
'bout your cheery disposition? Whilst I'm inclined to brood,"
"Well Sir" to me retorted, "You have yourself to blame,
For when Satan meets with humour, he tends to lower the flame".

Poetry Anthology No.2

H_2O

The pure crystal water, which springs from the hill
Births this H_2O fountain of sensual thrill,
Starts trickling and bubbling and laughing its way
Down the gently sloped mountain, past lambs at their play.
The trickle and splash as it joins with the stream,
Is the giver of life to the fishes that gleam
Darting hither and thither, or sleep in the shade,
As the water dance gaily, descending the grade.

Drained from the heather, the woods and the field
Must widen its banks to accept what they yield,
The croft in the valley, which the stream passes by,
Is the first man's abode that the waters espy,

The humans inside there are not full of greed
They only draw from it, as much as they need.
Tumbling onward past cattle and sheep
Through shade casting woodlands with pigeons asleep,

Where the wave bobbing moorhen and mud stirring grebe,
Fill this fluid oasis from which all creatures feed,
Meanders on gently 'tween reed clustered banks
Where the mayfly and swallow, tickle their thanks.
Peacefully onwards it wanders its way,
The wildlife abounding its banks at their play,
When it finally enters the regions of smoke,
Its freedom to wander is gone, in one stroke.

Wall clad and bridled, restricting its flow
Now it must follow where man makes it go.
Fresh water catchments extracting its flow,
Piping its lifeblood to cistern it, stow,
To pipe it and boil it, to filter and strain

But to drink of its liquor the humans disdain.
With caffeine they taint it and call it a brew,
Or hops are fermented till head it accrue,

Its sparkling transparency is clouded with soap
And dolly blue whiteness is added in hope.
When finally filthy, it's oozed down the drain,
And churned in dark tunnels whose stench it attains,
Where, polluted and rancid, its effluence spill,
Back to the river with much other swill,
The waters resilience has stood in good stead,
Soon the vile trace of humans, is thankfully shed.

Man's city, now past several miles in its wake,
The river returns to its healthier state,
But short lived the triumph, the miracle cure
For this bubbling river whose water now pure
Will soon again flow through another packed city,
And be ravaged once more without thought or pity,
To suffer again its life's blood re-letting,
Again drained away to douche man and his setting.

Ejected once more to the river's main flow
Where once gurgling laughter is now sultry and slow.
Struggle on seaward, sour, and filthy with gain.
Devoid of all life, near succumbed by the strain,
Where rocks, which should tumble, glisten, and shine,
Are bogged down with debris and covered in slime,
Where life in its waters is hampered and dim
Where once it was teeming and full to the brim,

Yet nature is kind, and her healing is sure,
For mile after mile she is cleansing and pure.
Reeds, which though stunted, they now may be found,

And even the water recovers its sound,
A strange new aroma is found on the breeze,
Is saline and tangy and not from the trees,
The ground now more sloping the river runs fast,
As though to escape from the thoughts of the past,

That salty aroma, is strong and inviting,
It now beckons onwards, the two soon uniting,
The river whose water is drained from the land,
Is cradled and succoured by the salt briny hand,
Together they mingle, caress, interflow,
The sea's cleansing bosom defines H_2O.

Widow's words

The number of days when I didn't, and many the
    nights when I could.
I'm counting the times when I hadn't, when I now
    know that really, I should.
For many and varied the reason, how futile and
    childish they seem,
Occasions that pass by like seasons, and moments
    that fade as a dream.

I beg you, dear friends, not like I did, I'm pleading,
    you don't let them pass,
For once the occasions are squandered, they don't
    come around more, alas.
Take courage, face up to each other, it's not such
    a hard thing to do,
Just hold and embrace when together, and mean,
    when you say, I love you.

Childs play

I canna gan doon yon way, an I canna gan doon that,
I canna play roond o'r way, 'coz I'm somewan else's brat.
O'r hoose is up on thet road, up top o' yonder hill,
But cars an motor riders scare us, 'cos they can kill.

I dinna want ta live here, all us kids feel the same,
Cos nowhere roond at o'r bit is it free ta have a game.
Yon bloke doon at the bottom an him up in the square,
They dinna have their own wains so they dinna ken ta share.

They wheek us fra the fitpath, they hoy us off the grass,
We canna play on kerbsides 'cos all they cars whiz pass.
The builders try they bestist, ta keep the road ways clean,
But wheer'l we kick wer fit-ba where is it safe a mean
I'm only one of meny, I'm only wee ya see,
But someday they whit chase us may have their ayn, like me.

Mind's eye

Some hours spent in wandering amongst the leafless glades,
By sparkling shimmering waters, whose crystal spumes cascade,
To tumble onward, downwards, in constant babbling flow,
'Mongst rocks, and roots meander, via pools and ponds to go.

The equinox of autumn, of daylight bare suffice,
Fast grip the chill of winter, of water still to ice,
Of grey clouds over shrouding, turn dark the earth below,
Soon downwards spiral falling, the world be white as snow.

See arrowhead formations, as birds are wont to fly,
Return from their migrations, head northwards cross the sky.
The boughs and buds from winter begin again to grow,
With colour glory flowing, to bloom the summer show.

How brief the kiss of sunshine, of bright and shining day,
To warmly bask in fragrance, where gamble lambs do play,
The young come into season, mature their mate to find,
Mankind aware of gender, will bear the need in mind.

Aware we are of seasons, of change within the year,
For each distinctive quadrant, bring music to the
   ear,
The cool of autumn's glory, the warmth of summer
   sound,
Are echoed in the story, of leaves upon the ground.

I feel obliged having suffered yet another birthday, to express my concern vis-a-vis the construction of another nuclear power station within the county, and God forbid, the construction of a radioactive waste depository for our waste and that of other countries. We do need a secure source of power to propel our industry and domestic services into the next century, to heat our homes and fuel our transport over land sea and air.
Oil will sustain us as a lubricant through the foreseeable future but not as a fuel and energy provider.

A Powerful Dilemma

My Grandad was blind, a staid Yorkshire bloke. his job in the gasworks turned Coal into Coke,

Others of that era were not so lucky, they worked down t'pit allus coughing and mucky,

I hope we're never again to resort, to pick and shovel to gain a result

Coal and steam hail industrial grime, we must move on from that torrid time.

Wainwright compiled his guides to the hills, pursued by many with time to kill,

Their trampling feet form a yellow brick road, whilst the hills bear the cost of their rambling load.

Tourists are vital and welcomed by the locals who, with pride justify

the hills and lakes and unique environ, yet fear to impose windmills thereupon.

The same can be said by the use of the sun, with panels and mirrors could power be won.

The sheep on the hills are sturdy and tough, and the stock in the fields are hardy enough.

which leads to the residue, commonly poo, diluted, fermented and added unto

Poetry Anthology No.2

we now call it slurry, produces a gas, which powers an
  engine whose product earns brass,
The basic ingredients be now odour free, as mulch and as
  compost no better there be,
This generated power each region's amount, together each
  unit inflates the account,
incorporated into the national grid, will credit the locals a
  couple of quid.

Waves have a power, phenomenal force, providing you
  first can milk them of course.
To capture the power of which they expend 'gainst
  beaches and objects above the ground,
or the rise and fall of the waves out at sea, can generate
  power that also comes free,
whatever fabric that can endure the force, or withstand
  the movement, from where the source
despite the corrosive power of the sea, the fabric selected
  immune it must be
Whoever unravels these quandaries, decree, be the energy
  saviour, relief, sets us free.
all nations can benefit, Britain the most, as long as that
  nation abuts to the coast.

Nuclear power, the miracle source, not the same as the
  bomb of course,
from rods of uranium the font of the heat, is steam
  generated which then turbines treat
and power generation is then assured, with its low cost
  per unit being quiet absurd.

Nuclear waste is right lethal stuff, a brown paper
  wrapping is not quite enough.
Initially stored under water, deep, pumped from the
  Florence mine, from a seep.
Items for storage deep underground are distilled, and

packaged and glasseous bound.
entombed in cement and even in lead, takes thousands
   of years before it is dead,
Secreted away deep underground, hopefully, where it
   won't ever be found.

The land around the Cumbria scene, is rocky and
   craggy and downright mean,
Totally what is Not desired. the opposite choice of what
   is required
to site a dump in this location, there must be better
   within the nation?
Clay is best, the rays to block, to hold inert the
   glasseous stock,
London's terrain seems to fit the bill, so, under there dig
   the hole to fill.

I was a member of the MOLES. Mines of lakelund exploration society. With thanks to Mr Ian Tyler and his wife Jean for many exhausting and enjoyable excursions down some of the 200 plus mines and quarries that can be found in the county, some date as far back as the Romans who mined for gold, silver, copper, lead,& tin. Many other products have been extracted from these hills, leaving the ground riddled with holes & fractured from frequent earthquakes that occur annually, The quake that hit Carlisle in 1979 registered 3.5 on the Richter scale
Surely this is sufficient grounds to justify to any intelligent body that Cumbria is totally unsuitable to house the Nuclear Waste storage dump.
This preamble has been my version of looking for a solution which faces us all. We live in a fabulous county and country, we must solve this dilemma very quickly, simply because I have grandchildren to whom I sincerely hope that I can hand over the mantle of life with a better prospect of a future than I started with in 1940.

On the Bridge

When you come to a quaint old humped backed bridge,
Which spans a sparkling stream,
You feel you want to linger there, and watch the waters gleam,
You may be in a hurry, and reluctant to delay,
Knowing all the time you should be going on your way,
But, something in the sound of water, purling over stones,
Full of lifting laughter, and of secret undertones,
Makes you want to stand, enchanted, lost as in a dream,
Fascinated, listening, to the music of the stream.

Joint Effort

My ailment dictates that I must be admitted
To submit myself for a joint to be fitted.
My right hip requires to be subject to change,
The old one is knackered, the fitting gone strange,
My home town of Carlisle was full to the brim,
So Hexham and Wansbeck have fitted me in.

To Wansbeck they sent me to be kitted out,
Strange land of the *Geordie,* of that there's no doubt,
The night staff assembled, prepared for their shift
These nurses are different, yet all with a gift,
Their footsteps they differ the *Left* from the *Right,*
And the noisiest trollies are saved for the nights.

The day shift departing with cheery farewells,
Give way to the time of the buzzers and bells,
Ignored whilst the conference of catching up, chat,
Acoustically Zero, the place where it's at,
Form a plan of campaign, their assault for the night,
Affecting each patient and bathe them in light.

The daytime tranquility fades with the sun,
And humour departs, gone the crack, gone the fun,
Imposed in its place the florescence of care,
Recounting of all the days antics they share,
Of drinking and shopping and travel by bus,
Of husbands, and children, and school homework fuss.

Poetry Anthology No.2

Date of birth and your name please? the pill-time request,
These pills are prescribed as a result of the tests,
Blood pressure, temperature, the pulse and its rate,
With catheter fitted, your bowel movement state?
"Now you wash your hands dear, your shoulders and chest,
Just don't be embarrassed, whilst we do the rest".

"Do you have any steps in the house that you live?
And anyone there who assistance could give"?
"In which case I feel that your progress is such,
That you staying in here will not vantage you much",
"I'll see you again in a further six weeks,
Spare pills and a bandage in case the wound leaks".

The worn out component has now been replaced,
And physiotherapy conditions embraced,
With patience and effort my limb should be sound
And hopeful enjoyment of agility found,
With freedom of movement and comfort regain,
A grateful farewell to the constance of pain.

To the surgical and nursing staff of Wansbeck hospital.
My sincere gratitude for your humour and character and
my grateful thanks.

Ena Hutchinson

Joy Complete

My heart still misses a beat, as I think
of the day when we were wed.
I skipped down the aisle
like a two-year-old
A perfect day ... complete

The Church was full of smiling friends,
who had come to share in our joy.
The sun shone down
not a cloud in the sky:
I believed it would never end.

Poetry Anthology No.2

Gilbert Hutchinson

"Will Not Come Back"

This poem is inspired by "Volverán las oscuras golondrinas" by the Spanish Romantic poet Gustavo Adolfo Bécquer (1836-1870)

Dark swallows will doubtless come killing
the injudicious nightflies with a clack of the
    beak;
but these that stopped full flight to see your
    beauty;
and my good fortune.....as if they knew our
    names-
they'll not come back. The thick lemony
    honeysuckle,
climbing from the earth root to your window
will open more beautiful blossoms to the
    evening;
but these....like dewdrops, trembling shining
    falling;
the tears of the day—they'll not come back...
Some other love will sound his fire word
    for you
and wake your heart, perhaps, from its cool
    sleep;
but silent,absorbed, and on his knees,
As men adore God at the altar, as I love you-
don't blind yourself, you'll not be loved like
    that.

Main Street Keswick 1985

Once in the shining street,
In the heart of a Lakeland Town
As I waited, behold there came
The woman I loved.

As when in early spring,
A daffodil blooms in the grass
Golden and gracious and glad
The solitude smiled.

Wedding Day

This was written after our wedding in 1986 when the taxi due to bring Ena to church failed to arrive. The Cathedral organist (Andrew Seiveright) entertained friends for half an hour before my bride eventually arrived.

There has fallen a splendid tear
From the passion flower at the gate,
She is coming, my dove, my dear;
She is coming, my life, my fate;
The red rose cries, 'she is near, she is near',
And the white rose weeps, 'She is late';
The larkspur listens, 'I hear, I hear';
And the lily whispers 'I wait'

She is coming, my own, my sweet;
Were it ever so airy a tread,
My heart would hear her and beat,
Were it earth in an earthly bed;
My dust would hear her and beat;
Had I lain for a century dead;
Would start and tremble under her feet,
And blossom in purple and red.

Poetry Anthology No.2

Ruth Kershaw

Full Circle

(or Wansfell (w)once more)

The year was 1948 –
School behind, work ahead –
A holiday with classmates three
Into Lakeland led.

The guesthouse was in Ambleside
And uphill; Loughrigg Brow,
Viewing heights and Windermere,
Breathtaking, awesome, WOW.

Rita and Eileen, Speg and me
With other toughs as well
Pulled on socks and sturdy boots
Then headed for the fell.

The day was hot, the leader fast,
And this our first true hike,
Pure bliss to find ourselves at last
On top of Wansfell Pike.

Steeply down to base again
Aching muscles stood no chance
As after dinner came the thrill
Of hectic Scottish Dance.

Poetry Anthology No.2

Becoming truly 'hooked' that week –
The sun, the mist, the rain,
By mountains mighty, fierce and wild,
I would return again.

Borrowdale, Grasmere, Bassenthwaite,
Eskdale en famille,
Coming back, year after year,
CHA houses right for me.

Eventually into leading on
Routes by now familiar
Through bracken, heather, stone and scree –
Oft times perpendicular.

Skiddaw, Glaramara, Bowfell,
Threading Gable's Needle,
Scrambling up the Langdale Pikes,
I should have been an eagle!

Years sped on, the pattern changed;
Cumbria then Pennine Ways
Long distance routes fulfilling
And challenging for days.
Retirement came, more leisure now,
Life one long jamboree –
Ramblers, U3A and more
Walks – ending up with tea.

And now, I fear, it's 'Can't keep up';
Strolling with fewer folk
For exercise and company,
The air, a view, a joke.

From on the bus at Kirkstone Pass
I spied an easy track
Wandering up to Wansfell's height
But this time from the back.

Heather was game – we started out,
That morning so kind hearted
And, sure enough, we landed up
Right where I once started.

2014
1948
62 years on.
FULL CIRCLE.

Poetry Anthology No.2

Rejoining.

In memory of Meryl & Michael (Eden Valley) : 2014

The unravelling
of the worn Jerkin
(wool from his flock –
spun and knit by her)
brought them into mind again.

Near to seventy years
they shared
and fifty plus
with us.
Our friends.

First wife,
then man:
fiercely met
by
Death.

Recycling
this yarn
into gloves
I clasp them.
Together again.

Poetry Anthology No.2

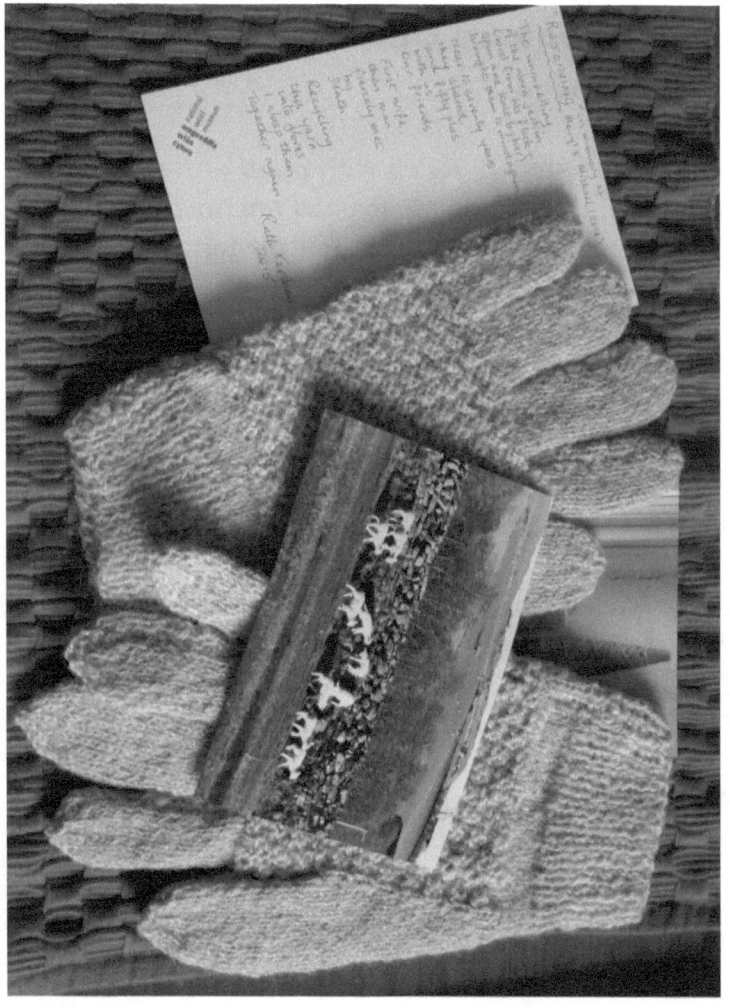

Back to Square One

(at Stones Barn)

All day we listened, toiled with mind and pen,
And then, that night, we feasted mightily.
We joked and laughed and then, by ten,
Felt to be lords of all eternity –
Yet earth was sad and we must put it right
To save it from its now predicted plight.
The rich against the poor, once more
(A problem met with many times before).
With voices strong and cheeks inflamed
We tried to find the ones who should be blamed.

There was a King with cash to spare
Who gave this wealth to courtiers one, two, three –
The first got ten, another five then (how unfair)
The last just one gold coin – Oh pity me!
The ten and five pursued a rise, the one a fall.
Surely the hardest parable of all!

Fatal Attraction.

*(for husband David. On the 2014 Poetry course at Stones Barn we were asked to write an **UN**-romantic valentine. He loved it...)*

'You draw me like a magnet!',
You said, as we
Lay in the ditch together.

You'd run into me,
Locked handlebars -
And down we flew.

Oh, why did I laugh?
If I was a fool then
I'm a bigger fool now!

The Strangers
(at Stones Barn 2019)

Arriving at the bus station with ten minutes to wait
She sat down to begin the quick crossword.
The man, pony tailed, can in hand, sauntered in,
Approached and asked `How old are you?
He had a few teeth missing.

What was all this about then?
Better rise to the challenge.
'87' she said.
'No!'
'I look more than 87?'
'No, you don't look 87.'
'And you?,
'50'
'A good age.'
'You think so?.'
'In retrospect, yes.'

That got him thinking – then 'What did you use to do?'
'Well, all sorts really but I've ended up a Methodist Minister.'
'Bloody Hell, you will have a degree in Theology!'
That got her thinking – what on earth did she look like!
And no,
She didn't have a degree in theology.
He was a chef en route to Newcastle
Three hour's journey with a change part way.

When the bus came in she found her seat,
Placed her bags beside her, continued the crossword.
Didn't need any more questions and answers
Especially now with others earwigging.

He sat behind her and carried on.
She listened but questioned less.
His elderly parents lived in Blyth where he was raised,
He was very fond of them.
They were chapel goers, fond of music;
He wanted to buy them a CD, but what to choose?
She suggested Mozart might be safe.
He scrolled his music on his smart phone.
Mozart wasn't there.

'I'm glad I've got you to talk to' he said.
'You're an Angel'.
That was a first – she certainly didn't feel like one!
Minutes later she melted -
'I suffer from depression' he sighed –
Relieved she had not shunned him.

The bus sped on, he now wanting to know what she
Thought of Socrates. Whatever next?
Carlisle at last!
A hasty farewell and murmured blessing
And off she dashed to get her connection,
Already in.

Pausing as she boarded,
She raised her hand to wave.
He was nowhere to be seen.

It is written:
"Be not forgetful to entertain strangers;
For thereby some have entertained angels unawares,"
(Hebrews 13 : 2 A.V.)

Into The Van..
(A Haiku – written in 2020)

Hands round waist push up,
Arms outstretched lower me down
From the too high cab.

The Man In The Van.

The man in the van,
Helpful and polite.
Or should I say
The men in ven?
More than one, you see.

The freezer was easy to handle. I was not;
Arthritic, short in leg, unbalanced;
Could slowly enter cars
But a van is high.
Firm hands around my waist –
Lower would have been better
But perhaps misinterpreted –
A push and up I go until
It's time to get down.
And he stood, solemn as a judge,
As I fell into his outstretched arms.

A week later, second,
The removal man
Faced the same dilemma.

Having downsized
There was furniture left behind
To sell, or give away.
The antique man came third.
Oh well....
And off I went again.

Number four – the joiner,
Old time friend who agreed that
The quickest way to get me up might be
A sharp pin in the rear –
But resisted.
Shoved me up fast
And smiled as he lifted me down.
My sympathetic man in the van

Oh Help

(Seeking support in 2018 during a time of stress over David's health problems we discovered that getting through to local health and social services took time and patience)

Late afternoon I phoned for help.
The receptionist took details,
Said she would ring back in the morning -
But didn't.

Come noon that day I tried again.
Apologies –
The helpers were
'All tied up'!

`Where are they tied?'
She went quiet,
Promised to ring back -
And this time did.

We are forever getting
Tied up,
Tied down.

Sixty years ago
We `Tied the knot'.

Now slipping.

Knotty Stuff (for David)

Sixty years ago today we `tied the knot'
With vows to love and cherish
`Till death do us part.

A rebellious schoolboy, you hated ties.
Perversely now, open neck in vogue,
You wear them with yes
A Windsor Knot.

Reef, Shipshank, Sheetbend, Granny –
Remembered from Girl Guides
To bind and make secure
And that safest for abseiling.
Bowline.

Is this the one we tied?

*2nd September 1958 – 2nd September 2018
(David died April 2019)*

Swim No More, My Lady

(A yearning look back to exhilarating swims at Crammel Linn in the Irthing Gorge near Gilsland. With Covid-19 swimming is on hold for most but, when allowed, this spot still attracts hundreds of people.)

In summer swimming pools attract –
Those out of doors are fun
With cafes and a few mod cons.
Restricting but I can cope.

Indoor ones where many learn to swim
Tempt me not at busy times.
Chlorine smell, tepid water, umpteen bodies
And oh - THE NOISE.

I was a wild swimmer, loving water,
Early strokes in the sea.
Rubber ring encircling waist.
Anxious father on the shore
Ready to wade in and fish out
Child in knitted swim suit (which sagged).

The baths win when it comes to getting changed –
Shower, shampoo, dryer, cubicle.
No sand between the toes,
Or lack of privacy.

But still the sea for me
Or lake or river – at one with nature,
Crammell Linn
So gloriously free!

Elderly and arthritic, I was invited
As guest to a private pool.
In the shallow end, lauching off
I went right under!
Not swimming but SINKING –
Swim no more, my lady.

Brampton Poets 2020

Poetry Anthology No.2

John S Langley

Surprise Package

It was only an envelope
in the back of a drawer
tucked away and forgotten

I recognised the address
took out the card, smelt
the familiar perfume, read

*'Happy Birthday, have a
great day, Love Mum, kisses
and hugs'.* It was a shock that

took me by surprise. Sparked
old memories. Happy. Sad.
My eyes began to water, unbidden

I held onto the card, ran my fingers
over the written words, felt
the ups and downs of a mother's hand.

***

Later I replaced it, put it back in its place.
It would wait there, cushioned,
ready to be discovered again,

by fresh eyes,
with fresh thoughts
on another day.

The Wheels on the Bus

The wheels on the bus go round and round
as I travel to school, uniformed, tie askew
wearing short trousers, smelling of youth
and vinegar, energetic in my direction-less-ness
looking out of the window, thinking of
maths, football, girls and lunch

The wheels on the bus go round and round
taking me into Newcastle, a younger brother in tow
fighting our way through the turnstiles to stand,
no seating here, holding on to the crowd barrier
all eyes following the black and white stripes
through the euphoria, the trauma of 90 minutes football
swaying wavelike with the crowd surges, dreaming
of fish and chips (with batter bits) on the way home

The wheels on the bus go round and round
as I gaze at my reflection, washed, shaven, clean
and smelling of Brut - I am irresistible!
The No. 263 or 264 crawls through the Manchester
drizzle that turns the roads into mirrors, reflecting lights
red, white, yellow. Impatient to be meeting friends,
and go prowling, predator-like across the dance floors.
Look out Manchester - here we come!

The wheels on the bus go round and round
transporting my wife and me from Portobello
into the city centre to watch Edinburgh Castle
light up with music and fireworks, pouring
sound into the night sky, flashing a crashing
rainbow of sparks into the heavens, shutting
off Princes Street, wondering how on Earth
we're going to get back tonight.

The wheels on the bus go round and round
round and round, round and round
the wheels on the bus go round and round
All day long

Carlisle Fish and Chips

It's the batter that brings you back
crispy and light with that unmistakable
crunch. The Tartare Sauce adds a twang
to the taste (if you need it). The chips are bathed
in malted vinegar (the only proper garnish
for proper chips). These are not French Fries these,
made from Cumbrian spuds, deep fried
and proud of it.

We're down the road from the coffee shops
with their cappuccino froth, full of expensive
expansive air. Nice for a sit down and a natter
but not for sustenance. This is where we talk
of books, family and who has just done what
to who and oooo...

But in the Fish and Chip Restaurant we eat in silence
surreptitiously wrapping a few chosen chips in bread
the butter dripping, dipped in sauce, trying to avoid
the glances

Look at those people they're too old for chip butties!

But we're not, we're in our shameless
chip butty public prime!
We're out of the closet...

I reach for a tissue to wipe the lavish greasiness
that has escaped from the edge of my mouth
and gaze down at the mushy peas
"you're next," I whisper.

Cat Sick

The cat had puked up on the carpet,
the beige one, freshly hoovered

Why should I be the one to clean it up?
I had given the cat its food
in carefully measured quantity

She had chosen to wolf it down
like there was a global shortage
or someone was about to steal it away

and then saunter over to the doorway
and throw it all back up again
giving a loud performance

of gagging, gasping. A guttural affair
of puking
and then just walk away

and creep behind the settee,
pretending that nothing had happened
pretending to know nothing about it

and start to lick her claws and
wash her face, ignoring the mess

You should clean up your own mess!

I shout at the cat (who doesn't move
or pause in her personal grooming)

Why should I clean up your mess?
I feed you, treat you for fleas,
get you serviced every year

and you do this to me!

The cat ignored me

so I went to the kitchen cupboard
got the paper towels, the sanitising wipes

This wasn't the first time!

and then I went down on my knees
and picked up the pieces of undigested food

wiped away the mess, washed away the stain
carried away the shrouded, squidgy remains
like the disembowelled remains of a mouse

and threw the evidence disgustedly into the bin.

Back in the lounge I looked at the cat

The cat looked at me ... imploringly

Hypnotised I returned to the kitchen
opened the pantry door, took out a sachet
of tuna with mackerel in jelly

gourmet deluxe

and somehow out-matched
went to her bowl and
replaced the food

She sat and watched me do it.

The Rapper

At the window there was rapping
while inside we were tapping
at our iPads and our tablets
at the ghosts of all our gadgets

Just a noise that caught us napping
just a rapping, tapping, rapping
as we sat without conversing
looking down at our diversions

Oh, the night had crept in early
and the atmosphere turned surly
cold was beating at the door
cold was seeping through the floor

We wondered what was all that rapping
we wondered what was all that tapping
on the expensive double glazing
the double glazing that's amazing

We wondered what would happen now
nothing said but with a raised eyebrow

decided with a gesture
to ignore the rapping, tapping
to ignore the tapping, rapping
and finish off this poem

then go and make a coffee!

P.S. It was a Blackbird pecking at the window, and then it went away.

First Steps

To walk the Wall
from end to end
what shall we see
what shall we learn

speak Wall
speak stones
tell of the years
the people you've known

stand tall
un-blistered feet
gracing new boots
slick with dubbin

protect well
my pink skin
unused to exercise
and the outdoors

I am ready

As never ready

Let's go!

Mary Queen of Scots

Let me lay this down
let me lay this down
for no one's eye except memory's
to prove that we can all
make mistakes

It was only two months
after the cold welcome
I'd given to her arrival.
A Queen and a prisoner
still making her royal demands

But as we spoke I began
to understand the hard
time she'd had of it.
The way her long awaited
son had been snatched from her

to be a two year old King
in her place and she, on
her walks outside the jail, with
her Ladies in the spring sunshine,
chattering and still able to smile.

I have to admit I came to respect
her resilient nature
and hoped that her cousin
would consider with Royal grace
her repeated entreaties

Poetry Anthology No.2

Note: *Carlisle provided a prison for Mary, Queen of Scots from 18 May to 13 July 1568. Francis Knollys was her reluctant custodian. She was never to be free again and was beheaded at Fotheringhay Castle on 8th February 1587 by order of her cousin Elizabeth I, who would never agree to meet with her.*

Bewcastle Cross

Such a cross, broken now
still standing, hewn from stone
erected

carved deep by skilled hand
in knotted designs full
of meaning

Four faces still carrying
runic inscriptions, praying
for prayer

Memorialising
our sins, our souls
Broken. Still standing

Poetry Anthology No.2

Reivers

It's dark and starless on this night
filled with the sound of the wind
rattling the shutters, wafting the
flames in the grate. The cattle
and horses are bedded below,
the door has been barred.

On short but sturdy steeds they clatter
over the hard-baked, stoney track-way
shadowed in their own high held torch
light, smelling of burning tallow, bearing
a grudge that also burns against a name
fuelled by repeated stories and tales.

This local vendetta's next chapter is about
to be writ in a burning barn and stolen cattle
and life lost. They say these are the Debatable
Lands but there is no debate in the air tonight
only blood lust for a doing, a new wrong to
right a past wrong, handed down and

repeated so many times that the truth is lost.
Nor is a truth needed where there is no law.
All that matters is that they are here, ready,
armed, determined. Their blood is up, it is
a night for reiving. The horses slaver against
their bits, and hooves and flames

begin to move. Musket and pistol are loaded
with shot and inside their Bastle a hand is
raised for hush as a family strains to hear
the sound of horses, the jangle of metal,
against the blowing of time's wind
that blankets our eyes from
the clattering of their fate.

Brampton Roman Camp

Silent now, the stones blanketed
in earth and years and green.
No more crash of metal
clash of tongues, guttural cries
rattling down the centuries

We drove past the school, turned
left, down the Old Church Lane
past the caravan park and parked
beside the farm. Today the ground
is carpeted in snowdrops.

Atop the old Roman fort a 12th
century Church still stands, the
silence of the graveyard broken
by a woodpecker drumming
amidst the trees.

300 year old headstones totter
but are still legible in the dim
shadowy light of a March day.
We walk to the far edge, past
yew trees of indeterminate age

and look down the steep slope
to the running sleekness
of the Irthing, carrying away
recent rains. We can see what
a vantage point this place must

have been with clear views
in all directions. A good choice for
a fort, a good choice for a church.
We can make out the old fort boundary,
mounded, grassed, attended by sheep.

Here in this place time rests on time,
life on life, and our own short visit is
dwarfed by the weight of those years.
As we prepare to leave I look up at the
bronze bell, atop the old church,
and am glad that, at least for today,
it lies silent.

A Bridge Too Far

I'm going to build a bridge, I thought, to stop me getting bored
I'll build it out of bits and bobs, I'll make it wooden floored
I'll concrete it on either side, so it's not washed away
not like the others that I've built, this one's here to stay

I got myself a ladder, of aluminium bright
it had the distinct advantage, of being rather light
I laid it lengthwise on the ground, and then from end to end
I covered it in planking, the type that will not bend

I am an Engineer, so know a thing or two
about structures and their tensions, their stresses and strainers too
so doing this was child's play, it went without a hitch
until I put it across the stream, the damn thing wouldn't fit

I pushed and pulled and remonstrated, it wasn't playing fair
It was about a foot too short, its length just wasn't there

The awkward thing refused to grow, not even one more inch
I'd have to face a change of plan, but that should be a cinch

My wife came down the garden, to see how I was doing
I rather wished she'd stayed upstairs, and carried on her sewing
I hauled the ladder out the stream, my features all aglow
'What are you doing?' she cried out, she really didn't know

'I'm rescuing this ladder' I said in feigned surprise,
'it's fallen in the water, you can see with your own eyes
it's tangled up in all this wood, it really shouldn't a ought'a'
I'm rescuing the pesky thing, I'm pulling it out the water.'

She gave me one of her special looks, my knees they turned to jelly
'Just get it done and then come in, "Bargain Hunt" is on the telly.'
I nodded as she walked away, my goose had just been cooked
I paused there in me wellies, how had the length'd been overlooked?

It's better to have tried and failed, than never
    tried at all
I would clear away all the bits and then could
    still stand tall
If after all I'd finished it, it would have looked
    bizarre
it's probably fair to admit, it was a bridge too far!

Actually I did build it – but I'm not sure how safe it is to cross!

The Dipper

The dipper bobs, pearls of water rolling
from his fine waxed plumage. Facing upstream
he is small, chunkily stubbornly stout
against the strong, fast waters, suddenly
disappearing under the water to hunt
the stone bed, silver-skin cloaked with trapped air,
his sharp beak and eager eye searches for stonefly,
caddisfly, mayfly, dragonfly nymphs.

A chestnut brown, white-chested feeder in
fresh water he is a welcome sign of
an unpolluted stream, dipping, bobbing,
darting, before taking low to the air
and returning in whirring flight to a bank-
-side nest of soft moss, grass and leaves
where sits a brooding female, patiently on eggs.

Impatiently listening for the sound
of the first fault lines of emergent life.

A Virtual Trip to Martindale

Drive down the M6, going south
turn off at Penrith and then right
refuel at Rheged under the
grass roof, on cooked foods, coffee and
stock up on local cheeses.

Now continue, following the
Eamont to pass bustling busy
Pooley Bridge full of tourist's camp-
-ing supplies and places to eat
if you take the time to queue.

Not like it was when I was young
the caravans, campers, yachts and
marinas on the narrow road
to Howtown where you hope not to
be pushed into walls by shiny
Audis, BMWs and Mercs

that travel at town speeds on the
country lanes. Relieved you reach How-
-town with its memories of close
shaves on school trips and scouting week-
-ends enjoyed, and on across

the bone rattling cattle grid, the
startled sheep, and on up The Hause
winding like a coiled snake, near vert-
-ical, hairpin corners, holding
on, fingers crossed to the top

of the ridge, finding the refuge
of St Peter's church lying in
dappled sunlight: but we are not
there yet, we are close but not quite
there yet. Onwards we must go

a little more, and down, to the
Howegrain Beck, the stone bridge, and park
Stop. Breathe. Pause. Dismount. We are here.
Take off your shoes, socks, roll trousers
to your knees and step bravely out
into the cold, clear waters

of past picnics, of yellow squares
of cheese and red sliced tomato
sandwiches and small pork pies and
crisps and sweet tea and games and sounds
of splashing, smells of heather

the hunting for frogs or newts or
dragons or anything your mind
can conjure in the moment, the
large rock, solid, looking on,
an Everest, presiding,

a pirate ship lookout, a test,
a memory, a memory
to return to in mind, when needs
be, when isolation bites home;

you rest at the pinnacle,
of a virtual journey, that
can be remade at any time
from any place, to bring a smile
as you look out and re-live this
from behind your closed eyes.

A watercolour scene of Martindale

Family Pieces

I don't know where my grandad
was from

I remember he coughed like water
rattling down a drainpipe

that he chuckled like a warm blanket,
crackling like burning twigs

that his head was growing past his hair,
a whale back emerging from the surf

that he drove at a single speed
crouching forward to accelerate
wondering why he didn't go any faster

I knew he'd been in a war
and hadn't enjoyed it

I knew he knew some songs
and could sing them
while I sat listening

Shouting 'Again!'
each time he'd finished
and my grandma would say

'Keep it clean, Tom
Keep it clean.'

***

And their dog Sally

who was made up of 57 varieties
which I thought was a good thing
but apparently wasn't.

She was a shaggy dog
with a big heart and a
licky, slicky, icky tongue

I couldn't say 'Sally'
when I was small
so I called her 'Waden'

but she came
just the same
wagging her tail

***

I don't know what Janet's dad
would have thought of me
calculating my intentions
with a Physicist's precision
hopefully getting them wrong.

I don't know my grandad Harold's story
from Cumbrian farming stock to
the North Eastern Railways
driven by steam
changing signals and points
collecting blackberries
from the scorched banking.

***

Poetry Anthology No.2

And how do I want to be remembered?
Warts and all, thanks
it's sometimes the warts that
are the most interesting parts.

As someone who was argumentative,
degree-ed, a man who loved being a dad,
bad tempered, obnoxious at times,
not always. Not boring
anything but that
please God, not boring!

There Will Come Another Spring

When buds appear again on the fruit trees
daffodils lift their yellow heads above
a carpet of white flowering snowdrops and
peacock butterflies flutter fresh from hibernation.

When the first blossom falls like snow on a soft breeze
the birds are bright in their breeding plumage
emptying seed from friendly bird feeders
and the owl calls in the clear daylight for her mate.

When bees awaken and seek pollen for new brood
blue skies feed the sleeping solar panels
frogs and newts return to the warming pond
and we wallow in double-digit temperatures.

When we anticipate the first swallow
darting through the air, hawking for fresh flies
while blue tits make claim to the old nest boxes
and despite occasional early morning frosts

the embryonic leaves thrust green from the branches
and you and I stand together and wonder
that, at last, there has come another Spring
There will come another Spring

Poetry Anthology No.2

Doreen Moscrop

Dawn o'er Blencathra

Soft and gentle, the silence of dawn,
A celestial winter's day has been born;
Bearing the message of this special dawn,
From the foot of Blencathra's great might.
Majestic beauty now grips my poor heart,
As dawn calls again for a new life to start:
Joy to all people who today play a part,
Drawn by this wond'rous sight.

Perilous ridges hang bare, raked with light;
Exploding rays burst from the heavens so bright;
On steep craggy shapes from your staggering height:
Sharp Edge has the power to enthrall.
Bright ribbons of silver in every ravine,
Streams cascade to the valley from waters unseen,
The spirit explodes with the wond'rous sight seen:
Stay imprisoned, my mind to recall.

Silver beams spread from the heavens above,
Calling me back to this mountain I love;
Over sharp icy crags once more free to rove,
Your fierce spirit held deep in my heart.
The pale sunset casts shadows o'er your many hills,
As enveloping darkness fills steep-sided ghylls:
Immortal as time, this sweet love for you wills:
    Ne'er more my quiet soul to depart.

The Winter Lullaby

Summer has departed, long gone the heated rays,
the nights grow ever longer; the hastily shortening days;
creeping winter leaves its tracks along the quiet ways,
ice fingers spread e'er outwards from guarded sheltering bays.

O'er fierce crags and gullies fine snowflakes drifting white,
to blanket over all that sleeps this special winter's night;
the timid creatures hide away before the frost dost bite;
visiting birds make final rounds afore their eternal flight.

The skies hang dark and heavy with clouds of black and deep;
hills in many shades of blue from winter mists do peep;
trees stand stark against the tarn, through boughs black shadows creep,
rough sheep upon the rugged hills for longer days to weep.

High on the cliffs above the vale the soaring
    eagles cry;
dark forms parade sharp silhouettes against the
    winter sky,
through fading light strange sounds resound,
    answering echoes do reply,
then all is stilled by approaching night and the
    Winter Lullaby.

The Wayfarer's Friend

Fingers of light, the sun's rays emerge above the rocky crags, piercing the hanging mists over the surface of the tarn. The quiet, broken by the gurgling beckoning sounds of my impatient friend beside me, eager to be on your way. Your darting between the peaty ledges is my cue to rise and leave this silent place, to begin our morning walk.

I rise, gathering my pack and stick, to begin our downward journey. Treading carefully I follow by your side, you trying to hurry my steps, rushing hastily over the stones, leaping, frolicking, playing the tune and that makes my excitement rise.

I quicken my steps trying to keep pace with your gathering momentum, the call of the skylark, the shriek of the crows on the cliffs high above join with your lilting music. Then I hear a new sound far below. You rush forward, frantic, suicidal towards the rocky ledge and hurl yourself over, disappearing from sight. With caution I approach the brink and witness your perfect dive into the reed encircled pool far below.

You call for me to follow but my climb down the steep rocks is slow and cautious. I catch up with you at last but you will not wait, eager now to join your companions, swelling your width, building your might and rushing ever onwards, plunging headlong between boulders, betwixt mossy banks to the valley floor below.

My steps quicken until I join you, your urgency quietens, slower now, my path levels, your surface settled as you contentedly glide over the gravel bed. Ahead shimmers the surface of the lake, you unhurriedly leave me, your journey over.

I say goodbye to my friend, my escort and thank you again for keeping me company.

The Geltsdale Shepherd

Forty years past he came to reside
in this quiet vale o'er the riverside
sharing this place with his happy young bride
a caring man with a gentle heart.
He came to know and love these hills
to carry with him those natural skills
nature's true gifts his whole life fills
this place has drawn, a shepherd born.

Over many long years he came to know
each lamb and ewe as they did grow
then after six years to the meadows below
harsh their life on the rough terrain.
With tender hands he did befriend
a troubled ewe with lambs, he'd tend
till late at night his time would lend
from early morn, this shepherd born.

To bring the flock down from the wold
the changing seasons, both warm and cold
to the dipping tub within the fold
with the devotion of man's best friend.
Those faithful collies so keen to guide
always stayed by the shepherd's side
the many tasks carried out with pride
on a crooked horn, leans a shepherd born.

Through wind and rain, come hail and snow
whatever the weather he'd always go
to rescue his flock before death's blow
did capture them upon the thaw.
When mists enfold, his way he'd find
locating the strays they'd left behind
guide them to safety when all were blind
needs no foghorn, a true shepherd born.

Those many skills with others to share
shearing the fleece, a lame foot to pare
a broken fence or a wall to repair
these talents, great gifts to bestow.
Proud of his family who share his life
a son's helping hand, a home-loving wife
his quiet existence in this world of strife
none did he scorn, our shepherd born.

The solitude found in those beautiful vales
following the sheep along well trodden trails
hearing the song of the sweet nightingales
ne'er happy away from Geltsdale.
The years slip by and friends come and go
but he'll never leave this place he loves so
his heart wanders immortal, his memory to stow
so many will mourn, that shepherd born.

The Mardale Shepherd

Until 1729, when the dalesmen were granted 'Right of Burial at Mardale', the dead of Mardale were strapped to the backs of horses and taken up the Corpse Road, by Mardale Common and Swindale for burial at Shap.

The hills around, the morning breaks
The valley still and clear
Since thoughts began and time moved on
My last journey drawing near.
The shadows grow, the mists move down
The fading of the light
Comes rain and cold, the lowering sky
Which darkens towards night.
One final round, my heart I leave at one
among my sheep
The sight remains, imprisoned now
Preparing my final sleep.
The horses wait, they taste the air
They sense the heavy load
To Shap, my final resting place
Over the old Corpse Road

Poetry Anthology No.2

Striding Edge

Is Helvellyn Mother Nature
in her final resting place
a cloak of scree protects her back
trees fashion a fringe of lace.
Red Tarn a jewel in her lap
Patterdale at the hem of her gown
two arms embrace this precious gem
the summit cairn her crown.
Her right limb is her mighty strength
strikes fear in the hearts of all
Striding Edge, a crest of naked rock
looming cliffs an encircling wall.
A walk along this narrow spine
stark rocks pierce ice and snow
running screes and unknown dangers
reverence to hold, excitement to flow.
Evening sunsets stage sharp silhouettes
walkers profiled upon the tor
as tiny shapes, a moving parade
riding nature's dinosaur.

The Winter Robin

I stop awhile to eat my fare
   then I see you waiting there
Red breast stands out against the snow
   your eyes, black beads see friend or foe?
Waiting, cautious, each one watching
   no movement now, my stillness matching
You hop towards me through the heather
   we share my meal, we eat together.
I talk to you, you seem to hear
   cocking your head you move quite near
No more crumbs, the food is done
   don't go away my heart you've won.
Then steps along the bank we hear
   listening now, I sense your fear
Strange sounds approach, you must away
   danger nears, you cannot stay
You dart away, then rise up high
   I watch you wing towards the sky
I thank you for these moments' pleasure
   you leave my mind with thoughts to treasure.

My Secret Tarn

I know you're there, I know not where
   my quest it is to find
Your surface still, beyond the hill
   that's pictured in my mind
You're all alone, your bed of stone
   your waters crystal clear
A trickling stream as in my dream
   I know I'm drawing near
I breast the rise, before my eyes
   your shimmering mass I see
Reeds all around, my vision found
   your peace does comfort me
I'll stay all day, won't go away
   'twill fill my heart with pain
Your secrets stay, till another day
   when I'll visit you again.

Poetry Anthology No.2

The Miner's Day

The straggling band, they climb the hill
   before the morning light
A gaping hole high on the moor
   inside as black as night
Endless dripping, echoes unchanging
   washing seams of shiny coal
Gathering pools deep in the earth
   gleaming black as a silky mole
Relentless cold and damp for poor reward
   on knees they crawl around
Dim candles flickering, on helmets they cling
   in those caverns underground
Dust and grime, they fill the air
   the blast a strange silence does leave
Blisters on hands burning from toil
   ever the dark burden to heave
Those little trucks now filled to the brim
   hauled with throbbing aching bones
Trundling their prize to the rim of the mine
   stumbling wearily over the stones
Work is done, evening light long gone
   no warmth from the sun to feel
Then brave the storm, the long walk home
   families wait with the evening meal
A life so short and so gruelling
   so harsh is the miner's plight
Like fathers before, sons to follow
   inescapable as day follows night.

The Magic Tarn

All alone
heart of stone
hurt inside
tears I cried
hills around
you I've found
surface calm
healing balm
dancing light
birds in flight
spirits rise
clear blue skies
joyous feeling
senses reeling
slowly healing
pain concealing
quiet to grow
peace to flow
The magic of this tarn.

The Carpets of Spring

The winter's done, the snow has gone
  now comes the springtime rain
The woodland floor, the rocky shore
  the hedgerows in the lane
An awakening sight, a sea of white
  in orchards sheltering care
The snowdrops play, Spring's on its way
  twill dress the branches bare
With white and gold and purple bold
  to attention the crocuses stand
Pointing high towards the sky
  as fingers on a hand
The daffodils, their petal frills
  sway in the gentle breeze
A yellow cloud, a statement loud
  to every eye does please
Near riverside, the trees would hide
  the fragile primrose lace
They nestle there, the dell to share
  with the tiny violets face
The land grows warm, a summer storm
  bright hues now fill the glade
Days grow long, the sun's rays strong
  and the Springtime carpets fade.

Poetry Anthology No.2

Jean Taylor

My Favourite Book

Oh how I long to read my favourite book
to forget about all my worries
and curl up in a cosy nook

To lose myself in words and text
where I don't have to stop and think
about the work that's coming next

nor think of life with all its sorrow
or wonder what may be tomorrow.

Poetry Anthology No.2

Stuart Turner

Beach Love

A cosy dinner by candlelight
Pushes back the years
When laughing friends and lovers met
'How do, are you well my dears?'

The girl from Aynsley Terrace
Who wore an orchid in her hair
Her father a rich and business type
With ice grains in his stare.

I feel so sorry for her though
With all the world her stage
A family with good but false ideas
She a bird in a gilded cage.

Ambition was the byword then
A car and Spanish hols
Ballet dancing and good music
Not rock 'n' roll and china dolls.

She joined the operatic group
Me the ATC
Pam was bound for Oxbridge
I a miner yet was free.

Still she joined a summer trip
Which took us to Whitley Bay
Enjoyed the beach, the fish and chips
As we laughed away the day.

At night till ten we had a beer
Went back to the beach us two
Indulged in frantic fumblings
To the sound of a sea bird's mew.

I never saw that girl again
Till now in this restaurant
No orchid but still as pretty
As she celebrated with her aunt.

She blushed, I stammered
'How are you?' She said 'Quite well.'
Then 'not really, truth to tell.'
But bowed her head and looked away.

The expectations had gone to pot
No kids, a bad divorce
I said I'd married young
Was blessed with boys of course.

The candlelight it flickered
We both looked wistful, sad
I took her hand on impulse
She whispered low 'I'm glad.'

We're best friends now, not lovers
That was never meant to be
But we'd felt the pangs of true love
In that seaweed by the sea.

Note: *The girl in question was my first heart's love.*
We were 16 and the story is true.

Poetry Anthology No.2

Autumn Fields

A tangle of meadow land
Quivering and dreamlike.
The brassy sun tilts earthward
As if in benediction lights
Living fields, soothes internal
hurts, caresses ancient human needs.
It is a madrigal, early autumn
Singing of growth and goodness
Rustic peace.

Visions of lord and peasant, yeomen
Contained within a green-gold tracery,
Timeless, essential, year on year.
Zephyrs of breeze, Atlantic born
Curdle stillness into a rippling
Golden sea and adds a sonorous
Whispering music.

The torment of that beauty
Remains months, years later
Extrapolated from the soup
Of memory, melds images into
A tangible legacy,
Something to
Treasure.

Early Winter Scene

Wings and petals still
Carved in scented air
Far horizons
Honking geese
Nature's panoply
Displayed.

People collecting
Treasures from hedge and copse
The smouldering piles
From the edge of town
Of leaf and grassy fires.

Yet, still potato pickers
In the sun bleached fields
Mid haulms
And dots of cornflowers blue
And few faded poppies too.

The acer's glow maroon
Under sun of burnished gold
And conkers fall
And split
To many a schoolboy dance.

Fruits aplenty
Hang low
Jabbering swallows
On the wires
And hedgehogs grub
In fallen leaves
A winter home to make.

As daylight fades
And dims
The watchful owl awakes
And marks
The helicopter spin
Of sycamore seed
And small birds' antics.

No one sees the wind
In gale
Or breeze
As it moves
Through wood
And meadow
Scattering twigs
And fallen leaves.

The air is raw and icy
Nipping cheeks
And finger ends
The first snow
Whirls and eddies
And white
Crowns holly berries.

Taken from an original artwork by Stuart Turner

Moorland

Stark against the skyline
juts a black finger
a cluster of odd-shapes
common enough in the lead dales,
an essential part of the scheme.

This one like a rotting
tree trunk, singled out by lightning,
black and cracked
with its own disuse,
brooding over a russet sea.

On closer inspection, we grasp
the real identity, a smelt mill,
reeking of decay, of former pains
breathing wretchedness in its stones
and trying desperately to disappear.

Small wonder, far from here
the spoils of hardship
saw Waterloo and Crimea,
bloodied innocent men's hands,
scorched agony in their minds.

Farmers had no choice,
men of means owned
this pile of debris,
from it gained their influence,
affected history, made me a poet.

For here it was I wandered,
whiling away my childhood
and unhinged the thoughts
that even then asked questions
shouted them into the wind.

Now the words echo again
swarm before my eyes
and beat upon my brain.
Curse these sick Satanic ruins
blotching my country's skin.

They stand hapless, present
A monument to man's
indifference, a reminder of
the disembowelled earth beneath
where blue-faced minions were spent

for the dubious rewards
of madness, of commerce,
insulting in their flush
uncaring in the scars
still here, a century later

as its master, modern man
didn't even clean up,
that's left to the clock
the sighing wild grasses
and the mind of a poet.

Poetry Anthology No.2

On Harrow Scar

My spirit lifted as the scent of
Wood smoke drifting up and across Harrow
Scar, Milecastle 49 in truth its
Stones blackened and cracked with
Centuries of weather and disuse,
Forsaken, forlorn.

Southward, across the Irthing Gorge
Cold Fell rises, filling the sky
And looking what it is, last bastion
Of the North Pennines, dun coloured
Bleak and inhospitable, England's last
True wilderness.

I sit and ponder the wild and
Familiar beauty, would the invader
Have had similar thoughts?
Or pulled the army tunic tighter
And cursed as rain, snow and wind
Growled down the hills' northern flank.

On or at this venerable spot
Laboured Romans, Dacians, captive
Cohorts from Gaul and Spain
Forever restless, always marching
To and fro, watching, waiting
Wary of the northern blue-painted Brigantes.

At my feet no marching cohorts, (though
ghostly figures were there in my avid
imagination)
Just the lonely delicate harebell lover
Of ancient stones, nodding in the northern
Breeze, peeling a silent requiem for a
Vanished people.

As I gazed a light snow shower
Brought a freshness to the air to all
So even the stones seemed cleaner, old
Leaves whispered like ghostly voices
Across the years, telling their stories
To those who had ears to listen.

I heard the distant tinkling of
Water below and watched a buzzard
Lift high above endlessly circling, watching
Over the ever changing hordes below
Closer, in tranquil mood the coo of a pigeon
And I felt contentment, peace.

My father, and my old headmaster
Would have loved this, been glad
After trying years of inculcation
To see me rapt, interested, appreciative
And my thoughts beckoned them but
They did not come, vanished like the Romans.

Turning, I saw the colour bled fields,
Heard a distant tractor coughing, struggling
For breath and sensed the passing of
An artist, maybe from Banks Farm, urgent
In the quest for bright wildflowers
To paint on a light kissed windowsill.

Oh! The magic in the air is music
The natural symphony of landscape
And history. Where they sat, I sit
Moved by the simple sights and sounds
In the early winter sun; my heart
Rejoices, another day is run, another wish fulfilled.

Death of a Friend

Some talk of status quo and rich success
For you a diamond rough, departed, gone
now to mellowed lands, a friend thus martyred
In the fires of life drawn by death's caress
To an undimmed stage; laugh now and impress
those nameless golden scribes of Heaven and there
tread avenues pure, carol the hallowed air
with rhyme far from the mill wheels of duress.
In nights of trembling peace when wise and shrill
the unseen owl calls from the drowsy hill,
hapless thought will turn to smiling memory,
for apart you gained immortality,
and through the void ring clear as midnight harp
to foster haunting pleasures bright and sharp.

Note: *A sonnet to a dear friend, in Shakespearian style.*

Winter Owls

The sun has dipped
Behind far grey hills
And a keen breeze
Scatters rotting leaves.
Gentle owls hoot
Glorying in this fine night
They quarter the green lane
Questing for food
And I listen, rapt,
Leaning on a tree
'too-whit, too-whoo.'

The moon like a lamp
Peeps through paper thin clouds
Glistening on fat bushes
And dark, sky seeking trees
In points of diamond light
A myriad will o' the wisps
Share some inane nocturnal dance,
And slowly, slowly
The mists of early night
Creep over the stiffening grass
'Too-whit, too-whoo.'

Poetry Anthology No.2

I inhale the winter
With its annual decay
Freezing fast in little mounds
And pungent whiffs of smoke
And wonder long, shivering
Where will we all be
Twelve months hence
Scattered through life's maze
Or still enthralled
Listening to winter owls.
'Too-whit, too-whoo.'

Note: *This was the result of listening to two Barn Owls quartering the lane behind our cottage.*

Lines Written to the Wind

My heart it soars with the wild wind
Over moorland and woods to the seas
Around me, the whole earth is shaking
To the stentorian roar of the breeze.

The heather and grasses are crouching
The bonny moorhen it is chaste
The twigs and dead leaves are jousting
As they whirl and dance o'er the waste.

I wish I could sit on the headland
Jutting out in the waves of Sulwath
Feel the sting and the salt sea tang
Of the ocean born wild wind's wrath.

Note: *Conceived on the summit of Talkin Fell one early autumn day as I was eating lunch.*

Poetry Anthology No.2

Taken from an original artwork by Stuart Turner

Talkin Fell

A modest height
As northern hills go
Yet high enough
To attract a sudden squall
Wind whipping hailstones
Into a vortex, stinging eyes
And ears and forcing even a few
Hardy sheep to run for cover.

Away to the north, beyond Cumbrian fields
The gleam of estuary on Scottish
Shores, washing Criffel's skirts
Sluicing up channels, bringing salmon.
To the south, all is grey and bleak,
Darkening horizons over
the merging fells around Croglin's outline.

A buzzard mews
As it dives on unsuspecting prey
A shaft of winter sun
Lights up the cracked grey and lichen spotted
Ruins of a cottage, waist high
In frozen grass, like a monument
To the blue-faced miners who
Earlier swarmed over these wastes.

The sun and thyme-scented air
Have gone, evaporating to other climes
A grey-brown, faded purple tundra extends
around. The only colours
Cotton Grass white and rare blooms,
Of Gentian Blue, in mossy hollows
Like sapphires, thrown by a passing prince
For starving travellers to find.

Upper Geltsdale

A journey to the very heart
Of the sparkling river Gelt
Walking fast, rushing
Not yet ready to stop
And contemplate. Gather
Breath and beauty,
That's all.

Higher I mount
Among heather, coarse grass
And bracken
And the lek lek lek
Of the bonny moorhen.

Till at last
I look back, panting,
Away at my feet lay
The world, habitation, Sulwath,
With its demands and
Obligations, its worries
Its crocodiles snapping
At my arse,
And laugh at them being scorned.

The invisible hordes,
Forgotten, neglected.
For it is a God-given
Fine day, larks are singing
And the best is yet to come.

Upper Geltsdale Winter

Icy boulders like old tooth stumps
Push through clumps
Of dead and frozen heather.

Hill sheep struggle
In the thin piercing wind
Even their favourite bush
Is beset by winter's blast.

The sky is steely grey
The whitest of suns is
Sinking like a torpedoed ship
Into the horizon of mud brown
Into the moors' frozen hulk.

Note: This poem and the previous one were written during my Lockdown on 26/3/20

Poetry Anthology No.2

Thank you for buying this Anthology

Now here is some space for you to add some poems of your own

Poetry Anthology No.2

www.ingramcontent.com/pod-product-compliance
Lightning Source LLC
Chambersburg PA
CBHW021105080526
44587CB00010B/396